From Welfare To Entrepreneur

The Entrepreneur's Guide To Success In The Marketplace

Rikita Watson

From Welfare To Entrepreneur
The Welfare Entrepreneur, The Entrepreneur's Guide To Success In The Marketplace

Library of Congress Control Number: 2018957235

ISBN-13:	Paperback:	978-1-64398-350-9
	PDF:	978-1-64398-351-6
	ePub:	978-1-64398-352-3
	Kindle:	978-1-64398-353-0

Printed in the United States of America

LitFire LLC
1-800-511-9787
www.litfirepublishing.com
order@litfirepublishing.com

CONTENTS

ABOUT ME

This book is based on my experiences in going from welfare to being an entrepreneur. Hopefully this book will provide life tools to encourage the reader that they can be an entrepreneur or enter into any kind of leadership position. This book follows the steps that I have taken during the course of my life, as I transitioned from being a teen mom on public assistance to a successful entrepreneur.

When I became responsible for someone else, I found a job and became dedicated to a position that made me feel hopeful. It taught me independence and responsibility, and I was able to provide for my son. However, my job was below minimum wage, and I couldn't really do too much with what I was making.

After being in the same place for years, I knew there had to be more that I could do to move my life in a different direction. I knew I didn't want to work for someone else, so I decided to take what I had learned and work for myself. When I started my business, I didn't know it would be successful. To my surprise, within months I was making a six figure income. I had no business school experience, college education, or loan from a bank. But God knew that being an entrepreneur was the path I should take.

INTRODUCTION

Being a single mother is hard, but being a young mother is even harder. This book is for those mothers that want the best for their children, who want there children to have a better life than they had. Having a child when you are young and don't have someone to help you can result in turning to the welfare system. But the potential for greatness is in you; you just need that kick start.

At the age of 18, I started working and landed a job where I was being underpaid and overworked. I was a faithful and responsible employee, but I also had bigger goals. I knew that one day I would own my own business. My early work experiences ultimately prepared me for my future as an entrepreneur. I had to trust in God's process for my life. I had to believe that things would work out for the best. Now I own my own business. Thinking back, I can say that things happen in our lives to create the person we will become.

This book will help you to look at your dreams, goals, and aspirations. This book is for the dreamer and visionary –

the one that people counted out, because of his or her life experiences. After reading this book, you will believe and dream again. This book will take you through the steps to finding your destiny or purpose in life. It will take you from being an underdog and will help you get to the top.

PURPOSE & DESTINY

Your Purpose

No matter what you are doing in life, search for your inner gift – the career path that you know you are supposed to have, something you find pleasure in doing, a path that makes you happy and blesses others. Find that inner voice that says you are on the right path to success. The more you pursue your purpose, the more you are fulfilled. Often, people feel frustrated by the everyday cycle. They feel as if their lives are not going in the right direction. But if you seek out your purpose, you will not feel frustration; you will be fulfilled.

There is more to life than just existing. We all have a purpose here on earth. I like to focus on this idea, because we each need to look beyond ourselves to find our purposes. When you walk in purpose, you may encounter some setbacks. Don't worry; setbacks are designed for us to achieve a strong comeback. Don't let your situation allow you to lose your focus.

Purpose is something that we are all born with. When people don't understand their purpose in life, they often try a little bit of everything. They work everywhere, take different classes, and even get multiple degrees, just to find out that they are not going to use any of their experience or education. Many people spend years performing jobs that they are unhappy with and unfulfilled by. When you find your purpose, you will find your fulfillment in life. Don't just settle for what you are used to, but reposition yourself.

God Gives Us All Gifts

We all have gifts we are born with. What you do with your gift is up to you. Sometimes we will see someone else pursuing an idea that we had. Although we thought of something new, we didn't pursue our own ideas. Could it have been because we didn't have the faith that we could do it? Or was it a lack of confidence? Were we just being lazy?

You have to identify what is stopping you from developing your dreams or having your visions come to pass. You do not have to follow the same life path that your parents or grandparents followed. If there is a cycle of failure, you can break it. I am the first person in my family to start a business, and I have been successful in it. I was a third-generation welfare recipient, but I broke the cycle. Instead, I became the first in my family to go from receiving welfare to being a successful entrepreneur.

Different Characters

I use many different characters from the Bible to show the different trials and tests we go through. As we trust the process, we receive our promise from God. As we stay focused and keep our eyes on God, He will bring us through those trials. Once Peter took his eyes off Jesus, he began to sink. Trials and tests are a necessary part of life. How we respond during those trials is the real test. We need faith in God to accomplish anything that is great. Be encouraged; your dreams will come to pass.

Being Chosen In Your Family to Do Something Great
A summary of how David was chosen to be King out of all his family

David was the youngest of eight brothers. David was chosen by God at a young age to be the king. David's father, Jesse, never even considered him. When the prophet came to anoint the next king, the oil wouldn't fall on any of David's brothers. David's brothers were older and had the physical stature that was expected in a king. They seemed to be a better choice for king, as far as cultural standards went. But they weren't God's choice.

God had a plan for David's life that was far better than He could ever have imagined. David was anointed king while he was feeding the sheep. This was not predictable, because David was not qualified for this position in the eyes of men. God chose him and that's what matters. God has a plan for you, as well. Trust in His plan, and you will find your path, just as David did.

Being In the Right Place to Prosper
A summary about Abraham leaving his father's house to go to a place where he would prosper

Abraham was told by God to leave his country and his father's house. He was instructed to go to a place that God would show to him. God made a lot of promises to Abraham, including how He would bless Abraham and make his name great. God promised that entire nations would serve him, so Abraham left his home with his wife and nephew.

This was a big test for Abraham. He was 75 years old when he moved. Abraham trusted God's process and understood that God had a purpose for his life. In doing this, Abraham received the promises of God and lived in a place of favor and blessings, a land flowing with milk and honey.

The Difference between Purpose and Destiny

Most people are confused about the difference between destiny and purpose. The two are not the same and shouldn't be confused. You are born with both a destiny and a purpose.

Purpose is what you were born to do, and it is especially carved out for you. I believe when you are following your purpose and doing what you are designed to, no one can do it better than you. You are made for your purpose in life. Your purpose can be anything from teaching children in Africa to building hotels in Guatemala. It can happen anyplace. You will find it, upon searching it out. Your destiny is your destination. Throughout your lifetime, you will make progress towards your destiny, in everything that you do.

Letters of Inspiration and Encouragement
Destiny

Reaching your destiny can seem challenging, because there are many obstacles that may occur while trying to get there. But you must still pursue it, and as you keep going you will see that everything is beginning to fall into place. You will start to understand why you had to take certain detours in life and overcome many setbacks. Eventually, you will understand why you had to take the road you took to reach your destiny.

There's a journey to get there and many stages to get through. Don't stop pursuing your dream. I know it doesn't look like it, but you are almost there. Obstacles can detour you, but God can reroute you. Your delay does not mean you will be denied.

Joseph and the Coat of Many Colors

Joseph's father, Jacob, loved him more than the rest of his children. His brothers knew that their father loved him more, and so they hated him. Joseph decided to tell his dream to his brothers, and they planned to kill him. His father gave him a beautiful coat with many colors, and that made them more outraged. They planned to sabotage his dream, so they threw him into a pit and sold him into slavery.

This brought him into Potiphar's house, where he became manager. When Joseph elected not to sleep with Potiphar's wife, she accused him of assault. Because of this, he was imprisoned. While there, he became the captain of the prison. He interpreted a dream, which landed him in a prominent position of power in the palace. There Joseph experienced victory over the adversity of his brothers.

Your Past Does Not Define Your Future

Your past doesn't define your future, and whatever hand that has been dealt to you does not matter. You can still grow from there. Get up and jump start your life, by stepping out in faith today. Never underestimate the power that you possess. Find what inspires you, whether it is in a book or magazine, music, etc. Whatever it is, find out where you draw your inspiration from, and continue to move towards your destiny.

People often get stuck in a certain place for years. There is no growth, because no one has inspired them to move. Surround yourself with people who inspire you to be your best, without being jealous of your growth.

God Has an Assignment

God wants you to exercise dominion and authority over the earth. Jesus could have forfeited his assignment to die for the sins of the world, because he was the son of God. He could have decided to enjoy the privileges that came along with being the son of God.

But God's purpose was to restore us back to being sons and daughters with the privilege of having access to His designs for our lives. Never be afraid to give up something for God, so that He can open new doors for you. God gave his son for all of us. Often, we have to do something we've never done, to get something we've never had.

Finding Your Passion

You need passion for whatever you want to accomplish. If you don't have passion, you may need to reconsider what you want to do. Sometimes people work in a field or chose a career based on the paycheck and benefits they receive. It is fine to want security, but our career choices should make us happy. If you enjoy doing a job, it will show in your work ethic. Others will perceive that you love what you are doing, and they will take notice.

No one should love what you do more than you. Love it so much that you would be willing to do it for free. No one should have to pay you to love what you do.

Section Summary

- Listen to your inner voice
- Discover your purpose
- Overcome detours and obstacles
- Understand the difference between purpose and destiny
- Discover your destiny
- Don't be stopped by your past
- Find your passion

Questions to Consider

- Do you know what your purpose is?
- Do you feel like there is something else that you should be doing?
- Are you satisfied with where you are in your career?
- What would you change about your life now?
- Do you know what destiny is?
- Are you fulfilling your destiny right now?
- What gives you inspiration?
- Do you feel inspiration coming from anyone you know?
- Do people always tell you that you should be doing something else?

VISION

Have Vision

Having vision causes you to think outside the box and create with your imagination. Visualization can also cause cycles of failure to cease. Your vision allows the power of your thoughts and imagination to manifest into reality. There's a scripture that says what a man thinks in his heart, so he is.

When some people visualize themselves doing something that they really want to do, things don't always happen right away. People tend to draw back and stop dreaming, when this happens. There's another scripture that says though the vision tarry, wait on it. Waiting for your vision is important.

Vision is Your Guide

Vision is your guide to knowing where you are going. It allows you to gain insight and revelation. Some people stay on the runway of life, never getting on a plane. They just stand on that runway and never take off. Visualize yourself on the plane that is taking off. Spread your wings and fly. Where do you see yourself in five years? Create a vision board and set your goals. If you don't have a plan, then you must be planning to fail. Stretch your imagination, and expand your mind to believe you can accomplish whatever you want.

Some people have short-term or long-term goals. It doesn't matter, but you have to start somewhere. Just begin to jot down some of your thoughts and ideas. You can even start with three or six month goals. Go over your goals on your vision board periodically. As you see progress, you can check off your goals and move forward.

If you don't have a plan or have something to work with, you will be unfocused. Seeing your goals daily and dreaming about them. But having a plan will ultimately result in you achieving the things you want. If you put in the work, your vision won't fail you. Work towards making your goals come to life, and then you will be able to see how far you've come.

Vision is What You Can See

Vision is when you can see something that nobody else sees. Your vision needs to be nourished and protected. That's why your vision or dreams should not be shared with everyone. Not everybody will understand your vision. Don't get upset when someone else can't see what you see. Your dreams belong to you. Even in relationships, the other person may not see what you visualize. Everything isn't meant to be shared. Protect your vision and be very discrete about what you share, because not everyone is meant to help your vision become reality.

Creativity and productivity will lead to your greatest growth experience. Having a creative mind is very powerful. You can gain great influence with your peers or acquaintances that are looking for growth in their own lives. Everyone wants to be around creativity; it's exciting and innovative.

Creativity brings about a greater desire to go higher and do more in life. We all want to do something we've never done before. Being a creative person stretches you and will cause you to break down barriers you thought you could never break. Don't get frustrated because you don't feel you can be creative; it's in you. Your creativity may provide the world with something it greatly needs.

Don't Stop Dreaming

Don't stop dreaming, even if you reach the level of success you have been working towards. What you put into life is what you get out of it. If you let laziness and procrastination take over, you will become stagnant. But if you remain motivated and inspired, you will keep moving forward. This is just the beginning of what is in store for you. The term "movers and shakers" is relevant. That's what you must become, in order to see things happen for you.

Staying motivated is the key to unlocking your creativity. You should not want to see yourself in the same place you were last year. Push yourself to the place you want to be, have a strategy, and execute your plan. This is how your dreams become reality.

Your Results

Your hard work and dedication will result in success. When you start building anything successful, you must be focused and disciplined to complete what you have started. Everyone will have challenges, but you must have the drive to push through adversity. Vision is something we don't usually hear too much about. But without vision, people perish.

How can you be successful? Vision needs to be at the forefront of what you want to accomplish. You must keep a picture of what you are building and how it looks in your mind, in order to complete what you are trying to accomplish. A builder needs to have a blueprint. Any successful person will tell you they have made a lot of mistakes, especially in the beginning of the building process. Some would say success can even be a bunch of mistakes turned right.

Vision Plans: Goals Example

This is an example of what your goals may look like:

SCHOOL – Finish next year, pursue a higher degree, take classes, etc.

HOME – Buy home within the next months, start a new renovation project, etc.

FINANCES – Fix credit, pay off balances, etc.

BUSINESS – Start a new business venture, create new business relationships, research business strategies, etc.

RELATIONSHIPS – Make new friendships, add connections, plan a family reunion, grow in relationships, take a family vacation, etc.

COMMUNITY SERVICE – Start a non-profit organization, feed the homeless, mentor children and adolescents, rehabilitate prisoners, etc.

PERSONAL – Buy a dream car, take a vacation, shop, donate to charity, etc.

Write the vision make a list of what you want to accomplish!

Section Summary

- Have a vision
- Believe in your vision
- Visualize your success
- Set short and long term goals
- Create a vision board
- Protect your vision
- Embrace your creativity
- Don't be afraid to dream
- Stay motivated
- Make a blueprint for success

Questions to Consider

- Do you have a vision for where you would like to see yourself in the near future?
- Do you consider yourself a dreamer or worrier?
- Are you afraid to share your dreams?
- Do you have someone telling you that you can't fulfill your goals or dreams?
- Do you have anyone that will support your vision?
- Can you see yourself in the place you want to be?
- Have you ever set goals and achieved them?
- Do you have goals set for this year? What are they?
- Do you feel you have a lot of challenges in achieving your goals?
- Do you know how to execute your plan for the future?

THE PROCESS

Process

I think anyone who is going to do something great will have to go through a process of being perfected. When you get to your destination and a storm arrives, you can't crack or quit.

You need to fulfill what you were born to do, and you will need longevity to accomplish your goals. You should never forfeit your dreams, because of the storms you will face. Trusting the process is to your advantage. You will build the character that will support you when all else fails.

Trust Your Process

Just about everything you do in life will involve a process. Don't get frustrated by the process; it is helping you become great. Be patient, and don't rush things. Your process is necessary for your development and growth. It will help you stay grounded and remain humble. As you elevate your life, your process will help you to mature. You will need this, as you ride your elevator to success.

Without putting work into your vision, it will only be a dream. You can't expect something to happen without working for it. You can easily sabotage yourself by waiting on things to fall into your lap. Talking yourself out of not following your dreams or not believing that it's the right time are also forms of self-sabotage. Don't allow others to talk you out of something that you have been waiting for in your life.

Self-Sabotage

Often, self-sabotage will occur when your behavior starts to affect your process and goals. The most common behaviors that lead to self-sabotage are procrastination, fear, quitting, and low self-esteem. You are not always aware that you are self-sabotaging, because the effects of your behavior may not be noticeable to you at the time.

Pay attention to what you do when opportunities present themselves, and what your actions are in those situations. These habits can be broken, but you must take action and get rid of any self-sabotaging behaviors that stifle your growth. I encourage you to get moving, so that you will not impede progress.

Section Summary

- Get through the storms
- Focus on longevity
- Trust your process
- Work for what you want
- Be cautious about self-sabotage
- Pay attention to opportunities
- Get moving

Questions to Consider

- Are you getting frustrated about your life?
- Do you feel stuck?
- Do you feel that you just need a push to get to the next level?
- Are you willing to work for what you want?
- Have you missed opportunities?
- Have you ever had any setbacks while perusing your dreams?
- Is discouragement stopping you from accomplishing your goals?

PATIENCE
&
TIMING

Letters of Inspiration and Encouragement
Believe

God wants us all to have ownership in our lives; that's a part of God's promise to us. Often, when we don't see God moving for us right away, we experience discouragement and doubt about what He promised. Sometimes you just have to show patience and believe God.

When God has you waiting, be patient. Be encouraged while you're waiting. Because you must wait, it simply means the time is not right or God has something better for you. Other times, He is meeting your needs, but you don't understand His plan. It is easy to get tired of waiting and stop believing, because you can't see what's happening. Believe all things are working together for your good.

Letters of Inspiration and Encouragement
Timing

When it is your time, you have to take action. Because many of us have missed opportunities to act, we have had to wait for the opportunity to present itself again. Timing has a lot to do with your success. That can mean several things. Timing may affect when you will get married, buy a house, start a business, move to another state, find your life's purpose, etc. Timing can make a big difference in many of the decisions we make.

One thing about timing is if you miss an opportunity, you may or may not have that opportunity again. So pay attention to timing, because there is a rhythm and sound to it. If you move with the rhythm, you will not miss anything. No one can stop you or block you. Even you cannot stop it, once you hear it and begin to move with it.

The Timing of God

A Summary of Abraham's Waiting on God

Abraham and his wife, Sarah, were very old when God promised them that they would have a child. Abraham was 100 years old, and Sarah was 90 years old. They were doubtful that it would happen, and they got tired of waiting. So they got one of the handmaidens to have a child for them. The child's name was Ishmael. But this wasn't Gods plan for them. After they had done this, their situation was a mess. They should have waited for God's plan to work.

Sarah did have a baby, whose name was Isaac. Finally, Abraham got the son that God promised, but God demanded that Abraham offer his son up as a sacrifice. Abraham's obedience was tested, but God had an alternative. A ram was found in the bush and accepted as an alternative sacrifice. In the end, God rewarded Abraham for being faithful.

Divine Timing

The Book of Ecclesiastes speaks about time and seasons. The divine timing of God is a super natural occurrence. When it is your time, there is a window in which you should act. You will feel a supernatural pull, when your divine time comes. Don't get caught up in the natural routine of life and you miss your divine timing. There will be many times in your life when you have to move in your divine timing. You will have to slow down and listen for the rhythm and move with it.

A Time for Everything
Ecclesiastes 3:1-8

For everything there is a season, and a time for every matter under heaven:

A time to be born, and a time to die;
A time to plant, and a time to pluck up what is planted;
A time to kill, and a time to heal;
A time to break down, and a time to build up;
A time to weep, and a time to laugh;
A time to mourn, and a time to dance;
A time to cast away stones, and a time to gather stones together;
A time to embrace, and a time to refrain from embracing;
A time to get, and a time to lose;
A time to keep, and a time to cast away;
A time to tear, and a time to sew;
A time to keep silence, and a time to speak;
A time to love, and a time to hate;
A time for war, and a time for peace.

Section Summary

- Know when the time is right to pursue your dreams
- Take ownership of your life
- Be patient
- Take action at the right time
- Pay attention to divine timing
- Follow the rhythms of your life

Questions to Consider

- Do you think that you make yourself a priority?
- Are you afraid to take ownership of your life?
- Would you move to another region, state, or country to achieve your goals?
- Are you in tune with your own life rhythms?

FAITH

Letters of Inspiration and Encouragement
Faith

Faith is something everyone needs. We need to have complete trust in God, no matter what situations we face. We sometimes say we have faith when we really don't. As soon as we lose a job or experience some kind of bad news, faith goes right out the window.

It is going to take faith to get you to the finish line, to get the job done, to keep going when everything seems to be falling apart. Even in our everyday lives, it takes faith to persevere, especially when you dream of doing something that has never been done before. Faith causes you to reach for something that is bigger than yourself and to achieve it.

Faith and Prosperity

You must have faith that whatever you do will prosper. If you plan on living a prosperous or productive life, you are going to need your faith. How do you expect to do anything without faith? Believe that God will send the provisions for your vision. Preparation doesn't cost anything; once you start to prepare for where you're going everything else will fall into place. Now is the time to put your faith into action.

Letters of Inspiration and Encouragement
Promise

When God makes you a promise, it will come to pass. He is faithful to his promises. There is nothing that can stop your promise, once God sets it in motion. He wants you to have whatever He promises, so much more than you would like to receive it. God's word has many promises in it, and He is waiting for you to access them through your faith. You must trust in His promise, and He will supply your every need. There is nothing that will be withheld from you, because He is a good father. He loves you and wants the best for you.

Section Summary

- Have faith
- Trust in God
- Persevere when life is difficult
- Faith leads to prosperity
- Trust in God's promise

Questions to Consider

- Do you struggle with faith in visualizing your dreams coming to pass?
- Are you afraid to put your trust in God?

FOCUS

Stop Procrastinating

Don't procrastinate. Why put off till tomorrow what you can do today? Follow your inspiration. You are already in agreement with your purpose and destiny. Keep moving towards your vision and goals. You must see yourself being successful in whatever you are trying to achieve. Visualizing makes things happen.

Become Knowledgeable

Keep reading up in whatever area you want to be successful in. Research your interests and master them. Be so knowledgeable about what you're doing that people will come to you for information and understanding. You are an asset and not a liability. You are the innovator and the one with new ideas in your chosen field.

Be Determined

You will need much determination to push yourself towards your goals. Do not see yourself as stuck in your current location. Push yourself where you are trying to go, and make no apologies for your determination.

Have a Strategy

You need to have a strategy. Have a date in mind regarding when you want to start the new project or business venture. Research how long it will take you to bring this concept to life. Think about how much it will cost and where you will launch your idea. Think about whether you will need someone to help you achieve your goals, and start looking for the right person to help you get started.

Get What You Want

You don't need man's validation if God puts the desire in your heart. Go and get what you want! The world is at your fingertips. You need to reach up and grab what you want. Everyone's experience is different. Just because something didn't work for someone else, doesn't mean it won't work for you. You don't need everyone's advice; try not to lean on man to guide you through. Trust God and the process; then focus on what it will take to get you to the place you are trying to go.

Push Yourself

Push yourself past your own limits and don't focus on the negative. You will have negative thoughts and doubts. You will worry about whether or not you may succeed. Cast those thoughts down and always focus on the positive. Think about the possibility of being successful.

If it looks like you are failing, don't focus on the negative. Keep having faith. The place that you are now is not permanent; you may not be there tomorrow. Tomorrow might be a better day. Sometimes you have to encourage yourself, look at yourself in the mirror, and tell yourself failure is not an option.

Stay in Pursuit

Stay in pursuit of your destiny. Do not let anyone or anything keep you from going higher and wanting more out of life, in business or even in relationships. Keep a positive outlook on things, even when things seem to look like they are going the opposite way.

You determine your own success, not anyone else. Continue on your path, focus, and don't sweat the small things in your life. They will detour you from your goals. Everything doesn't always have to be perfect. You can take your time getting wherever you want to be.

Have the Eye of the Tiger

The eye of the tiger is about getting knocked down but getting back up again. The Bible says a just man falls seven times and gets back up. Don't be afraid of falling down; just don't stay there. Be unstoppable, unshakable, and keep your eyes on the prize. Turn your dreams into reality. Keep your faith and press toward your goals. Look at that target and believe in yourself. Your aim will be on point, and you won't miss. Stay focused on your goal, and don't give up.

Eventually, you will see everything you've been working for come to pass. The victory is in your hands. Your determination, perseverance, faith, and hope will pay off. You will reap the benefits of this fight.

Positive Affirmations

Your success starts with your mindset. What you believe about yourself is what you will display outwardly. Always maintain positive affirmations about your life, goals, dreams, future, and destiny. Be careful of what you say and allow others to say to you. Remove yourself from negative situations. Always maintain your faith, even if things are going in the opposite direction of your dreams. You can determine your own destiny.

Success doesn't mean you have to finish high school or even college. It simply means you have an idea that you want to manifest. I'm not saying drop out of school or don't attend a college or trade school. Just take the limits off yourself. Trust in God. You can do whatever you put your mind to do; success is already in you.

Sometimes It Looks Too Hard

Sometimes you may feel like accomplishing your dreams and goals or fulfilling your destiny looks too hard. But you have a cheerleader alongside you; that is God. Search for that inner voice that is pointing the way. In certain cases, achieving your goals may mean you have to move. Some dreams are easier to achieve in a certain location. You may feel more inspired in a different place than where you are currently living.

Breaking Cycles

There are many people that have a problem progressing. They set goals, but don't reach them. Their plans go out the window. They don't understand why they cannot get from one place to the next. When you feel like something is stopping you, you are going in a cycle and not accomplishing your goals.

Cycles can impede your growth; this can happen in business and also in your personal relationships. Observe your life and see if things are falling into place for you. If not, you need to pray and confront whatever is stopping you. You can't achieve your goals if you are not willing to confront those issues in your life.

Keep Your Mind Sharp

Keep your mind sharp, always thinking of another plan and expanding your mind so that you can ultimately take over the world. You need to believe in yourself and your brand. Know that no one has a better brand than you, even if the person next door is pursuing the same goal. If you need convincing in your own abilities, how can you convince someone else to believe in you?

Section Summary

- Don't procrastinate
- Become knowledgeable
- Be determined
- Have a strategy
- Know what you want
- Push yourself
- Stay in pursuit of your dreams
- Have the eye of the tiger
- Use positive affirmations
- Don't give up
- Break cycles
- Keep your mind sharp

Questions to Consider

- Would you like to focus more on yourself?
- Do you always put everything else before yourself?
- Do you have a difficult time sticking to your commitments?
- Do you procrastinate or do you get things done?
- Are you an early person or a late person?

SUCCESS

Your Success

Your success is not based upon how much school you attend or how many degrees you receive. Success can happen as a result of believing in what you want. When you aim for an accomplishment or achievement, you can break down barriers that are designed to keep you in the same place. Look at what is in front of you, and don't be afraid to step outside of the box.

Opposition is the brick and mortar towards building something great. Use that opposition to build your empire. Overcoming obstacles gives you the fortitude and patience to continue. The most successful people have a drive and the mindset of "I can, and I will." Maintain your vision, and put your ideas to work. That's how empires are built; that is how people succeed in business today. Your ideas and influence can bring about global wealth.

Success and Money

Most people equate success to money. However, this is not true. If you were born into money, the definition of success would be different. Success can have many different meanings, and you may feel you are already successful. Happiness might give you a sense of success. Just because you have money, does not automatically mean you are happy. Some of the wealthiest people are very unhappy. Working hard to accomplish your vision and goals is fulfilling. Making progress towards those goals will make you happy. Being successful, however you define it, will make you feel accomplished.

Expansion and Progress

Success is often based on how you expand and progress in achieving your goals. Success is not determined by how big your bank account is. People view success differently, and many people go through life thinking that they can't be successful. If you are one step closer to your dreams and goals, then you are on the path to success.

Many people are afraid of what it takes to be successful. They plan to fail, because they don't believe that they can be the one you see on television or in commercials, whose brand you see in stores, or whose music you hear on the radio.

King Solomon's Story

King Solomon's story is very relevant in teaching us how to use wisdom to make the right decisions concerning our everyday life. Solomon asked God to give him wisdom to judge his people. God granted Solomon's request, so he ruled and managed his people successfully. It is important for us to allow God to guide us in our affairs as Solomon did. Solomon knew that he was creating a temple for ruling and that he would need wisdom.

Wisdom helps us to problem solve and judge even the smallest matters in our lives. Acting with wisdom allows us to make good decisions in our families, jobs, communities, churches, etc. We need the abilities Solomon used to succeed in our everyday lives, especially as we begin the building process to live a life of success.

Jesus Tells the Parable of the Talents to His Disciples

Jesus tells the story of a man who goes away on a trip. Before this man leaves, he entrusts three of his slaves to invest his property; to one he gives five talents, to the second he gives two talents, and to the third he gives a single talent. The first two slaves doubled their money. They gave the original investment and their profit to the master when he returned. The third slave, however, buried his talent in the field instead of trying to make a profit.

The master was pleased with the first two slaves, but disappointed with the third. He disciplined the third slave and cast him out into darkness. This is an example of being unproductive and not using your gifts, or talents, wisely. We are expected to invest in ourselves and become productive citizens.

Section Summary

- Believe in what you want
- Overcome obstacles
- Success does not equal money
- Continue to expand and progress
- Use wisdom
- Invest in yourself

Questions to Consider

- What does success look like for you?
- Do you feel like you are being hindered form achieving success?
- Do you feel you are not qualified to reach your goals?
- Do you feel like you have ever reached a level of success?

INFLUENCE

Using Influence

Very successful people are usually people of great influence. They have influenced others to listen, follow, and trust in their words and deeds. Influence is a good characteristic to have. It leads to wealth and success. You should seek to influence people. Our former leader's influences have changed the course of our world. Be a world leader, by influencing and impacting those whose attention you already have.

Quality Relationships

Successful people surround themselves with like-minded people and have no time for those who want to drain them. You will need to keep a clear mindset so that those creative juices and new ideas can flow. You should break away and set yourself apart from those who are not good for you.

Surround yourself with people who can help you create a positive atmosphere. This will help you to make good decisions, sign the right contracts, buy the perfect property, define your brand, create merchandise, etc. Search for quality relationships that will fit you best. Creating a positive atmosphere will help you to be great and succeed.

The Greater Good

Make sure that the success you are working for is for a greater good. On your way to the top, build up others by inspiring them to fulfill their dreams and destiny. Being successful is not always about you being in the spotlight and feeling a sense of achievement. You can help build confidence in others.

Stay humble and be grateful for what God is doing for you and where he is taking you. Be thankful for the many roadblocks and detours you had to endure. Stay faithful in working towards fulfilling your purpose and destiny in life. There is no rush to get there, as long as you handle your business along the way. There are many stages to success and to your destiny, so make sure you're not chasing your dreams for the wrong reason.

Make sure that you are passionate about what you are doing, as well as contributing to the greater good. Do you love what you do? If you feel that you can do it forever, you won't get bored or tired and quit.

Section Summary

- Influence others
- Use your influence to change the world
- Surround yourself with positive people
- Remove negativity from your life
- Create a positive atmosphere
- Work for the greater good

Questions to Consider

- What type of influence would you like to be on other people?
- What changes would you like to make in the world?
- What negative influences can you remove from your life?
- How can you surround yourself with positive people?

ENTREPRENEURSHIP

Being an Entrepreneur

Though being an entrepreneur can be very glamorous, there are winds that blow from time to time. Be sure to hold on, because it can be a bumpy ride. Your business can be up today and down tomorrow. It is up to you to stay consistent. Being an entrepreneur is not for the faint of heart. You need to know which way the ship is sailing and take charge.

Being an entrepreneur isn't for everyone. If you choose to be your own boss, life can be very exciting. Every day is a new adventure. You get to build a company from scratch; you are the director and you have control regarding where you want your business to go.

To become a great entrepreneur, you must be a great leader. Entrepreneurship requires a willingness to expand or stretch yourself. You must be willing to learn. There are many sacrifices you will have to make. You will put in many long days and nights, which will cause you to sacrifice some of your personal time. This is not a normal 9 to 5 job. You will have to be available when no one else is. You will be required to complete tasks and meet deadlines when everyone else has gone home. Entrepreneurship requires dedication to your purpose and completion of assignments, regardless of the circumstances. Faithfulness is the key; you must stay committed to what you have set out to do.

Make no apologies for how you run your business, because no one else knows what it will take for you to be successful in business. Everyone's work ethic is different. What works for others may not work for you.

When you are an entrepreneur, you must live a life of creativity. You are expected to create the wealth you need for the lifestyle you want to live. Nothing is handed to you; you have to go and create what you want. Don't be afraid of being told no, because eventually someone will say yes. Sometimes we have to wait for things to manifest. Sometimes you need to wait for things to happen or work in your favor. Don't look at the negative because, as long as you keep your faith, things will turn around and work for you.

Building Your Brand

When building your brand, stay consistent. Don't copy what you see someone else doing, because everyone is different. In order to be successful, you have to change things up a bit. Know what your limits are and how far you want to go. Have a clear outlook on how you want your business to be set up.

Consider all the pros and cons if you are considering entering a partnership. Some people can really be of help to you in developing and marketing your business or brand. If you decide to bring in another person, that is fine. It could be very beneficial in growing your business. One person doesn't know everything, so having another voice can be very helpful.

Experience is your best teacher, but there are people who may be more experienced and knowledgeable than you are. I am all for building a team of people who can carry out your plan and get the job done. However, this is not for everybody. You don't want to get into a position where there is a clashing of wills. You need to consider how much focus and discipline each person brings to the table. One person may be more motivated than the other. Have a vision for what you want, and be sure to set up a system that will work for you.

Creating Your Next Stream of Wealth

Entrepreneurship is great, but it should not be limited to doing one thing. People are creating different streams of wealth, producing multiple sources of income. You can work your gift, not only in one area, but in multiple places. In our modern society, you will probably want to have multiple streams of income. Because the economy and all industries have cycles, you will want a variety of revenue options. The marketplace is wide open for new ideas, new products, and new inventions. Expand your capacity to create; don't be limited by one audience, create your next stream of wealth.

Ultimately, we should strive to have multiple streams of revenue. We should use all our gifts to make a difference in the lives of others. So keep your mind sharp, always consider other plans, and expand your mind so that you can ultimately take over the world. You are the best at what you do. You need to believe in yourself and your brand. Know that no one has a better brand than you. Believe this, even if the person next door has the same product.

How to Discover Your Next Season

You will need to discover your next season of your life, so that you can move forward into it. Thank God for how far he has taken you. Refocus and strategize about whatever you want to do next. This is something that needs to be done often, especially if you are in business and things that use to flourish have now begun to be stagnate.

Don't be discouraged, because your next season is right around the corner. During your next season, you will open the door of opportunity to enter into your next phase of life. It's time to embrace your new season and what is next for you, so that you can write the next chapter in your life.

Section Summary

- Stay consistent
- Be a great leader
- Be willing to sacrifice
- Make no apologies
- Embrace your creativity
- Build your brand
- Consider a partnership
- Explore other revenue options
- Don't limit yourself
- Always move forward

Questions to Consider

- Would you like to own your business?
- Can you see yourself being an entrepreneur?
- Are you afraid to step out on your own as an entrepreneur?
- If you decide to be an entrepreneur, would you try partnerships?
- What steps would you take to start your own business?
- What would be your timeframe in pursing your entrepreneurship?

DEFINITIONS

Accomplish- To bring to its goal or conclusion, carry out, perform, finish

- To complete
- Something that has been achieved successfully
- An activity that a person can do well, typically as a result of study or practice
- Skill or ability in an activity
- Expertise, skill, skillfulness, talent, ability, mastery, capacity, proficiency

Achievement- Something accomplished especially by superior ability, special effort, great courage, heroic deed

- The act of achieving; attainment or accomplishment
- Something completed successfully, goal reached
- Performance, fulfillment, success, victory, triumph

Action- The fact or process of doing something, typically to achieve and aim

- A thing done, an act
- Armed conflict
- The events represented in a story
- A gesture or movement
- A manner or style of doing something

Administration- The process or activity of running a business or organization

- The officials in the executive branch of government under a particular chief executive
- The action of dispensing, giving or applying something
- The management of any office, business, or organization
- Supervision, an act of dispensing

Aim- Point or direct, at a target

- Point direct, train, sight
- Have the intention of achieving
- Purpose or intention; a desired outcome
- The direction of weapon or object at a target

Afraid- Fear or anxiety; fright

Attention- Notice taken of someone or something, the regarding of someone or something as interesting or important

- The action of dealing with or taking special care of someone or something
- A person's actions intended to express interest

Audience- The assembled spectators or listeners at a public event, such as a play, movie, concert, or meeting

Barriers- Anything built or serving to bar passage as a railing, fence, or the like

- Any natural bar or obstacle

- Anything that restrains or obstructs progress, access
- A limit or boundary of any kind

Believe- Accept, as true, feel sure of the truth, confidence in, trust in, consider truthful

- To suppose or assume, understand
- Believe in
- To be persuaded of the truth or existence of

Brand- A type of product manufactured by a particular company under a particular name

- The promotion of a particular product or company by means of advertising and distinctive design
- A brand is a product, service, or concept that is publicly distinguished from other products, services or concepts so that it can be easily communicated and usually marketed

Building- A structure with roof and walls

- The process or business of construction, edifice, erection, construction
- Construct by putting parts or material together over a period of time
- The process of constructing, shaping, developing or forming a particular thing
- Increase the size, intensity, or extent of

Business- A person's regular occupation or trade

- An activity that someone is engaging in
- A person's concern
- The practice of making one's living by engaging in commerce
- Commercial operation or company
- Trade considered in terms of its volume or profitability

Commitment- The state or quality of being dedicated to a cause, activity

- An engagement or obligation that restricts freedom of action
- A pledge or undertaking
- A promise to do or give something
- Dedicating yourself to something, like a person or cause

Committed- Dedication and loyalty to a cause, activity, or job; wholeheartedly dedicated

- Obligated, bind, a contract committing to complete a project
- Committed in relationships
- To pledge or assign to some particular courses or use
- To put into charge or trust

Confident- Feeling or showing confidence in oneself; self-assured

Consistent- Acting or done in the same way over time

- Unchanging in nature, standard, or effect over time
- Compatible or in agreement with something

Creativity- The use of the imagination or original ideas, especially in the production of an artistic work

- The ability to transcend traditional ideas, patterns, relationships, or the like
- Meaningful new ideas, originality, progressiveness of imagination
- The process by which one utilizes creative ability

Cycle- A series of events that are regularly repeated in the same order

Discourage- Cause to lose confidence or enthusiasm

Delay- Make someone or something late or slow

- Postpone or defer an action
- A period of time by which something is late or postponed
- To put off to a later time
- To impede the process or progress of, hinder
- To act of delaying, to put off action

Determination- Firmness of purpose

- Purposeful
- The process of establishing something

- The controlling or deciding of something's nature or outcome

Detour- A long roundabout route taken to avoid something

- Taking a long roundabout route to visit somewhere along the way
- A circuitous way or course, especially one used temporary when the main route is closed
- A route that is different from the ordinary, often used when the direct route cannot be used

Development- The act of process of developing growth

- A developed or advanced state or form
- The part of movement or composition in which a theme is developed, or unfolded

Dreams- A state of mind in which someone is in daze or trance, haze

- A cherished aspiration, hope, goal or aim, intention; intent, wish, yearning
- Indulge or daydream of something typically greatly desired

Economy- The wealth and resources of a country or region, especially in terms of the production and consumption of goods and services

Encourage- Give support, confidence, or hope

Entrepreneur- A person who organizes and operates a business or businesses, taking on greater than normal financial risk in order to do so

Environment- The surroundings or conditions in which a person, animal, or plant lives or operates

Expand- Become or make larger or more extensive

Faith- Complete confidence in someone or something

- Strong belief in God, based on spiritual apprehension
- A system of belief
- A strongly held belief
- Confidence or trust in a person or thing
- Belief without proof
- The obligation of loyalty or fidelity to a person, promise, engagement
- Belief in anything, as a code of ethics, standards of merit
- The observance of this obligation, fidelity to one's promise, engagement
- Christian Theology, the trust in God and in his promises as made through Christ and the scriptures by which humans are justified or saved

Finish- Bring to an end; complete

Fulfill- Bring to completion or reality; achieve or realize something desired, promised, or predicted

Frustrated- Feeling or expressing distress and annoyance, especially because of inability to change or achieve something

Focus- The center of interest activity

- An act of concentrating interest or activity on something
- The point of origin of an earthquake
- Pay particular attention to
- Concentrate

Forfeit- Lose or be deprived of as a penalty for wrongdoing

Gifts- A thing given willingly to someone without payment, a present

Goals- The object of a person's ambition or effect, an aim or desired results

- The destination of a journey
- An observable and measurable end result, having one or more objectives to be achieved with in a more or less fixed time frame
- The score made by this act
- A point making the end of a race
- Objective, aim, end, target, intention, intent, plan, purpose, ambition, aspiration, wish, dream, desire, hope

Greater- Usually or comparatively large in size or dimensions

- Large in number, numerous

- Notable, remarkable, exceptionally outstanding
- Of outstanding powers, having unusual merit, very admirable
- Enthusiastic
- A person who has achieved importance or distinction in a field
- Of high rank, official position, or social standing
- Much in use or favor
- Enthusiastic about some specified activity; great persons, collectively

Growth- The process of increasing in physical size

- Expansion, extension, progress, advance, development, spread
- The increase in number and spread of a small or microscopic organism
- The process of developing or maturing physically, mentally, or spiritually
- The process of increasing in amount, value, or importance
- Something that has grown or is growing
- Something that has increased in size, a gradual development

Impede- Delay or prevent by obstructing; hinder

Innovative- Something new or different

- Featuring new methods, advanced and original
- Introducing new ideas, original and creative thinking

- The process of translating an idea or invention into a good or service that creates value or for which customers will pay
- Deliberate application of information, imagination and initiative in deriving greater or different values from resources

Knowledgeable- Facts, information and skills acquired by a person through experience or education, the theoretical or practical understanding of a subject

- Being aware of something
- Understanding, mastery comprehension
- Awareness of familiarity gained by experienced of fact or situation

Limited- Restricted in size, amount, or extent; few, small, or short

Marketplace- **A**n open area in a town where a market is held

Moves- The way something moves or works, or the effect it has on something else

Movement- An act of changing physical location or position or of having changed

- An arrival or departure of an aircraft
- A change or development

Moving- Producing strong emotion

- Going in specific direction or manner, change position
- Change or cause to change from state, opinion, sphere, or activity to another
- Take action
- Make progress, develop in a particular manner or direction

Ownership- The act, state or right of possessing something

- State of owning something
- The state, relation, or fact of being an owner
- A group or organization of owners
- Possession, right of possession, freehold, proprietorship, propriety rights, title
- The state or fact of being an owner
- Legal right of possession; proprietorship

Partnership- The state of being a partner or partners

- An association of two or more people working together
- A business or firm owned and run by two or more partners
- The contract creating this relationship
- An association of persons joins as partners in business
- A form of business where two or more people share ownership

Persistence- Firm or obstinate continuance in a course of action in spite of difficulty or opposition

- The continued or prolonged existence of something
- Having continued or permanent persisting

Plan- A detailed proposal for doing or achieving something

- An intention or decision about what one is going to do
- Decide on and arrange in advance
- Acting on, doing, proceeding to do, develop in advance
- An orderly or step by step conception or proposal for accomplishing something

Positive- Consisting in or characterized by the presence or possession of features or qualities rather than their absence

Press- Move or cause to move into a position of contact with something be exerting continuous physical force

- Apply pressure to something
- Move in a specified direction, pushing
- Squeeze or crush
- Forcefully put forward to persuade or force
- Make strong efforts

Process- A series of actions or steps taken in order to achieve a particular end

- A natural or involuntary series of changes
- Walk or march in procession

Procrastinate- Delay or postpone action, put off doing something

- To put off to another day or time, delay
- To defer action; delay
- Prolong, postpone
- To put off doing something, especially out of habitual carelessness or laziness
- Postpone doing what one should be doing

Produce- Make or manufacture from components or raw materials

Productivity- The state or quality of producing something especially crops

- The effectiveness of productive effort, especially in industry, as measured in terms of the rate of output per unit of input
- The quality, strategy or fact of being able to produce
- The quality, state or fact of being able to generate, create, enhance or bring forth goods and services

Progress- Forward or onward movement toward a destination

- Advance or development toward a better more complete, or more modern condition

Promise- A declaration or assurance that one will do a particular thing

- Assurance, pledge, agreement, commitment, contract, covenant

- Give good grounds for expected or expecting a particular occurrence or situation
- Announce as being expected to happen
- Assure someone that one will definitely do, give or arrange something, undertake or declare that something will happen
- Pledge someone, especially a woman to marry someone else; betroth; contemplate the pleasant expectations of

Purpose- The reason for which something is done or created or for which something exists

- To intend design
- By design, intentionally
- With intention, meaning or plan
- An intended or desired result; end; aim goal
- God's intended plan; what he had for you to carry out

Pursue- Continue or proceed along a path or route

- Seek to attain or accomplish especially over a long period
- Engage in an activity or course of action
- To form a mental image of, make visible to the eye

Pursuit- An effort to secure or attain

- Act of pursing
- Any occupation, pastime, or the like which a person in engaged regularly or customarily

- An activity of specified kind, especially a recreational or athletic one

Push- Exert force on something or someone typically with one's hand, in order to move them away from oneself or the origin of the force

- Hold and exert force on something so as to cause it to move along in front of one
- Move one's body or a part of it into a specified position especially forcefully or with effort
- Press
- Cause to reach a particular level or state
- Move forward by using force to pass people or cause them to move aside
- Exert oneself to attain something or surpass others

Results- A consequence, effort, or outcome of something

- Occur or follow as the consequence of something
- Have a specified end or outcome
- A satisfactory or favorable outcome of an undertaking
- Verdict, decision, outcome, conclusion, effect, reaction

Setback- A reversal or check in progress

Start- Come into being; begin or be reckoned from a particular point in time or space

Stifle- Make someone unable to breathe properly; suffocate

Strategy- A high-level plan to achieve one or more goals under conditions of

- A plan of action or policy designed to achieve a major or overall aim
- The art of planning and directing overall operations and movement in a war or battle
- A plan for movements during battle

Stretch- To draw out or extend to the full-length extent

- To hold out, reach forth, or extend
- To length, widen, distend or enlarge unduly
- To extend, force or make serve beyond the normal or proper limits
- To recline at full length
- To extend over a distance or area or in particular direction
- Elasticity or capacity for extension

Success- The accomplishment of an aim or purpose

- The attainment of popularity or profit
- A person or thing that achieves desired aims or attains prosperity
- The outcome of an undertaking specified as achieving or to achieve it's aim

Target- A person, object, or place selected as the aim of an attack

- A small round shield or buckler
- Selected as an object of attention or attack

- An object or result toward which efforts are directed

Timing- The choice, judgment, or control of when something should be done

- A particular point or period of time when something happens
- Plan schedule, or arrange when something happens
- Perform an action at a particular moment

Trust- Firm belief in the reliability, truth, ability, or strength of someone or something

- Confidence placed in a person
- Have faith or confidence
- Acceptance of the truth of

Vision- The faculty or state of being able to see

- The ability to think about or plan the future with imagination
- A mental image of what the future will or could be like
- Imagine

Vision Board- A tool used to help clarify, concentrate and maintain focus on a specific life goals

- Any sort of board on which you display images that represent whatever you want to be, do, or have in your life

Visualizing- Form a mental image of; imagination, dream, picture, envisage

- Make visible to the eye
- To recall or form mental images or pictures
- To make perceptible to the mind or imagination
- To render visible, as in an image or representation
- To produce an image or visual representation of by radiological

Work-Hard- Great deal of effort or endurance, working hard to be successful in business

- To work with energy and commitment, diligent
- Something or someone that is diligent in laboring and puts effort into doing and completing tasks